1950s

Enriching farm soil with fertilizers and using irrigation to water the soil helps to create a green revolution that produces more food.

1928

Penicillin, the world's first antibiotic, is discovered by Scottish scientist Alexander Fleming. It is made from penicillium, a fungus found in soil.

2014

Part of a hill east of Oso, Washington, collapses, sending soil and mud sliding across a river and burying 49 homes. It is the single deadliest landslide in U.S. history.

1930s

A decade-long drought dries out the ground in America's Great Plains so much that hundreds of millions of tons of soil blow away.

2015

A new antibiotic called teixobactin is discovered in soil.

1953

An antibiotic called vancomycin is discovered in bacteria found in soil.

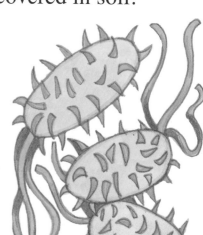

What Is Dirt?

Dirt is the main component in soil. While they share some similarities, dirt and soil also have many important differences. Unlike soil, dirt does not contain any living organisms—it is basically just dead soil, and we cannot grow plants in it. This book will focus on soil.

Soil is the crumbly top layer of Earth's land surface. It is a mixture of gritty particles of rock, air, water, living organisms, and the remains of dead plants and creatures.

Soil is essential for most of the plant life on land. It soaks up water like a giant sponge. It acts like a filter, cleaning water that moves through it. It also affects Earth's atmosphere, because it absorbs some gases from the atmosphere and gives out others.

There are lots of different types of soil, and scientists have made maps showing where they are. The colors on these maps represent the many different types of soils.

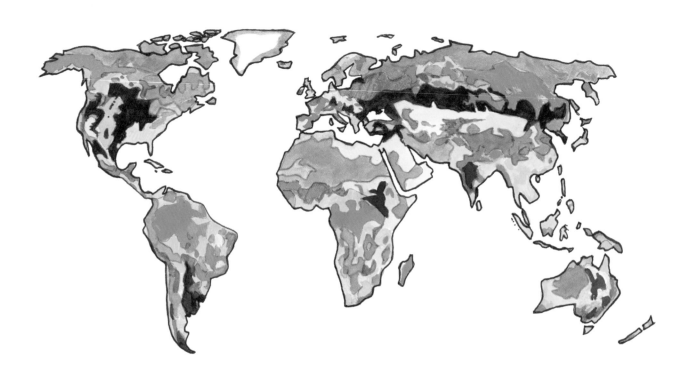

Author:

Ian Graham earned a degree in applied physics at City University, London. He then earned a graduate diploma in journalism. Since becoming a freelance author and journalist, he has written more than 250 children's nonfiction books.

Artist:

Mark Bergin was born in Hastings, England, in 1961. He studied at Eastbourne College of Art and specializes in historical reconstructions, aviation, and maritime subjects. He lives in Bexhill-on-Sea with his wife and children.

Series creator:

David Salariya was born in Dundee, Scotland. He has illustrated a wide range of books and has created and designed many new series for publishers in the UK and overseas. David established The Salariya Book Company in 1989. He lives in Brighton, England, with his wife, illustrator Shirley Willis, and their son, Jonathan.

Editor: **Jacqueline Ford**

Editorial Assistant: **Mark Williams**

Cover artwork: **David Antram**

© The Salariya Book Company Ltd MMXVI
No part of this publication may be reproduced in whole or in part, or stored in a retrieval system, or transmitted in any form or by any means, electronic, mechanical, photocopying, recording, or otherwise, without written permission of the publisher. For information regarding permission, write to the copyright holder.

Published in Great Britain in 2016 by
The Salariya Book Company Ltd
25 Marlborough Place, Brighton BN1 1UB

ISBN-13: 978-0-531-21488-6 (lib. bdg.) 978-0-531-22438-0 (pbk.)

All rights reserved.
Published in 2016 in the United States
by Franklin Watts
An imprint of Scholastic Inc.

A CIP catalog record for this book is available from the Library of Congress.

Printed and bound in China.
Printed on paper from sustainable sources.
1 2 3 4 5 6 7 8 9 10 R 25 24 23 22 21 20 19 18 17 16

PAPER FROM
SUSTAINABLE
FORESTS

You Wouldn't Want to Live Without™
Dirt!

Written by
Ian Graham

Illustrated by
Mark Bergin

Series created by
David Salariya

Franklin Watts®
An Imprint of Scholastic Inc.

Contents

Introduction

What if we didn't have any soil? It's hard to imagine. If there were no soil, our world would be completely different. The ground would look different and many of the plants and trees we know today would disappear.

Soil supplies a surprising variety of raw materials for making things. Without soil, we would have none of these useful materials, and there would be no muddy puddles to splash in! If soil had never existed, life itself would have developed differently on Earth and we humans probably wouldn't be here at all. That's an amazing thought, isn't it? No soil, no humans. In fact, most life on land would not exist. There are some bad things about soil, too, but even so, you wouldn't want to live without it.

SOIL HAS numerous uses. Plants grow in it. It provides raw materials for building. It has supplied medicines, cosmetics, cleansers, and artists' pigments (colors). It's useful for burying things we want to keep out of sight, like water pipes and trash. Animals use soil, too. Insects, worms, moles, rabbits, and many other creatures live in it.

Where Does Soil Come From?

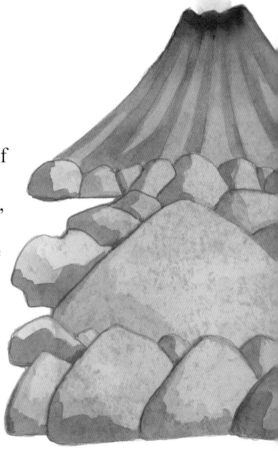

When Earth was a newly formed planet billions of years ago, it had no soil. Its surface was solid, bare, hot rock. Then it started to cool down. This cooling caused tiny cracks in the rock. Water and ice got into the cracks and made them bigger. The hard surface slowly broke up into smaller and smaller pieces of rock. The first simple plants appeared on the land more than 400 million years ago. When they died, they broke down and their organic matter mixed with the rock dust. This mixture started to change the lifeless rock dust into soil. Wind, rain, and rivers moved the soil around and spread it across Earth's surface. Then bigger and more complex plants grew in the soil. Green plants changed the atmosphere by adding oxygen. Without soil, Earth's surface would have been bare rock, there would have been no fields or forests, and the atmosphere would have been toxic.

AS WATER moves rocks around it bashes them together. This wears them down to a rounded pebble shape. Tiny pieces of rock knocked off them form the grit that helps to make soil.

GLACIERS are slow-moving rivers of ice. As they slide downhill, they grind up the rock below them. This creates vast quantities of rock dust and larger pieces of rock that will later form new soil.

Look, it's new soil forming!

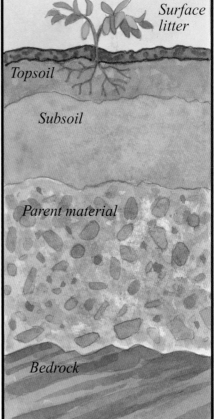

Surface litter

Topsoil

Subsoil

Parent material

Bedrock

WIND blows sand around, sometimes in giant sandstorms that travel great distances. As soon as the sand settles, plants and creatures move in and begin changing it into soil.

SOIL forms in layers. Broken-up pieces of bedrock called parent material supply the gritty pieces of rock in soil. Most of the organic matter (decomposing plants and creatures) is in the topsoil. The layer below is called subsoil.

Types of Soil

Soil is not the same everywhere. There are different types of soil in different places. Soil type is the result of the bedrock that forms it, the current weather, and the varied types of living organisms that move into it and change it. All soils are a mixture of sand, silt, clay, and organic matter. Sandy soil lets water drain through it easily. Fine silty soil turns to mud when it gets wet, but it blows away easily when it dries out. Clay soil is dense and heavy, and it can be molded like modeling clay. Peaty soil contains a lot of organic matter.

HEAVY RAIN and flooding are bad for soil. The organic matter and nutrients (food) are washed out, turning the soil into muddy sludge. Water also keeps out air needed by living organisms.

THE IDEAL SOIL for growing plants is called loam. Loam is a mixture of organic matter and equal amounts of sand and silt with a little clay. It feels soft and crumbly. Loam is good for growing plants because it holds water and nutrients, but it also allows excess water to drain away. Fertile farm and garden soil is loam.

Test soil to see what type it is by rubbing it between your thumb and fingers. Sandy soil feels gritty. Silty soil feels smooth and soft. Clay soil feels smooth and sticky. Peaty soil is springy and contains a lot of water.

THE ACIDITY or alkalinity of soil is called its pH. Neutral soil has a pH of seven. Acid soil has a pH number lower than seven. Soil with a pH number higher than seven is alkaline.

WATER DISSOLVES the nutrients in soil. This makes the soil acidic, neutral, or alkaline (the opposite of acidic). If you put a plant in soil that is too acidic or too alkaline for it, the plant won't grow very well and it may even die.

MOST PLANTS grow best in neutral soil (neither acid nor alkaline), but some plants have a definite preference. Rhododendrons (at left) are flowering plants that grow best in acid soil. Lilacs (at right) prefer alkaline soil.

A Home for Life

Lots of creatures make their homes underground in soil. Many of them also help to produce new soil. Bacteria and worms break down dead plants and change them into organic matter called humus. Humus holds water and nutrients that plants can take up through their roots. Soil's ability to hold water also slows the downhill flow of rain into rivers, helping to prevent floods. Soil also attracts bigger creatures looking for food and shelter. Some of them, including moles and rabbits, live in tunnels and burrows underground. This network of interconnected animals and plants feeding off each other is called the soil food web. Without soil, a lot of creatures would be homeless and there would be more flooding!

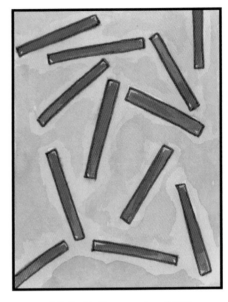

VIRUSES. Soil contains billions of viruses. A virus can't reproduce but it can invade other living cells and trigger them to copy its genes. Some viruses cause diseases in plants and animals.

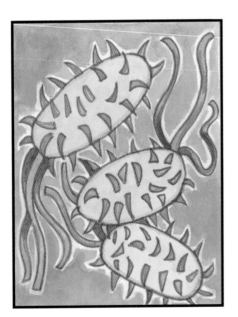

BACTERIA (left). Large numbers of single-celled organisms called bacteria live in the soil. They are vital for healthy soil. Some bacteria break down organic matter. Others enable plants to take in nitrogen from the air and use it as food to help them grow.

PROTOZOA (right) are single-celled and larger than bacteria, but still microscopic. They are able to move through soil, and they feed on bacteria, other protozoa, fungi, and organic matter. Each of them can eat up to 10,000 bacteria a day.

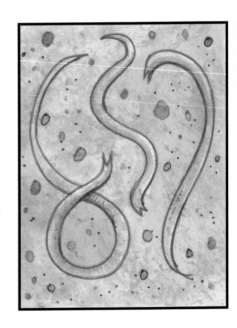

HEALTHY SOIL is full of life. Most of it is too small to see without using a microscope, but there are lots of larger organisms, too.

Top Tip

Soil can harbor harmful organisms and substances that could make you sick. Wash soil off your hands as soon as possible, and definitely before you eat. Don't forget to scrub under your fingernails!

Fungi

Insects

Microbes

WORMS. Earthworms as well as microscopic worms called nematodes live in soil. They feed on other organisms and dead plants. Their tunnels allow water and air to move through the soil.

INSECTS. Ants, beetles, and other insects spend at least part of their lives in soil. Grubs that you find in soil grow into insects.

MICROBES. Microscopic organisms in soil are often called microbes. They include viruses, bacteria, algae, protozoa, and fungi.

11

What Can You Make From Soil?

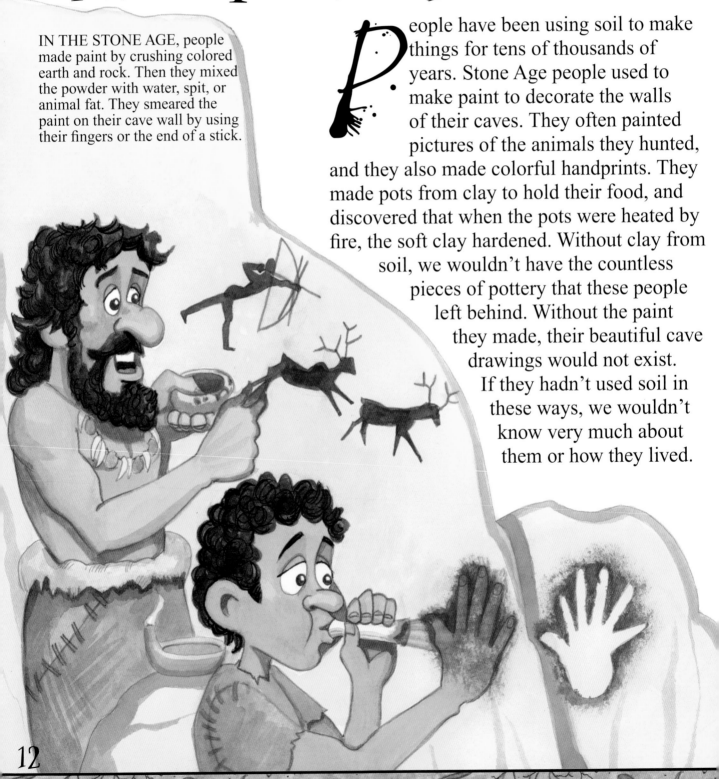

IN THE STONE AGE, people made paint by crushing colored earth and rock. Then they mixed the powder with water, spit, or animal fat. They smeared the paint on their cave wall by using their fingers or the end of a stick.

People have been using soil to make things for tens of thousands of years. Stone Age people used to make paint to decorate the walls of their caves. They often painted pictures of the animals they hunted, and they also made colorful handprints. They made pots from clay to hold their food, and discovered that when the pots were heated by fire, the soft clay hardened. Without clay from soil, we wouldn't have the countless pieces of pottery that these people left behind. Without the paint they made, their beautiful cave drawings would not exist. If they hadn't used soil in these ways, we wouldn't know very much about them or how they lived.

CHINA'S FIRST emperor, Qin Shi Huang, was buried with thousands of statues of warriors to protect him in the afterlife. The life-size statues were made of terra-cotta. Terra-cotta means baked earth. It's a type of fired clay.

How It Works

When clay is fired, it changes. At a temperature of about 2,190 degrees Fahrenheit (1,200 degrees Celsius) the clay particles fuse (join) together. This is a permanent, irreversible change.

GRINDING UP earth can make a variety of pigments, from black and dark brown to red and yellow. Other colors can be made by mixing pigments. Pigments with umber, ocher, and sienna in their names are earth pigments.

Cassel Earth Raw Umber Burnt Sienna

Raw Sienna Red Ocher Yellow Ocher

Brown Umber Vegetable Black Van Dyke Brown

Red Oxide Mexico Yellow Burnt Umber

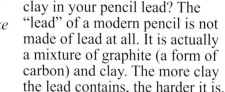

SOME AFRICAN peoples grind up earth to make a red paint called ocher. They mix the paint with fat and smear it on their body and hair. It stops their skin from drying out and cracking. It also stops mosquitoes from biting them.

DID YOU KNOW that there is clay in your pencil lead? The "lead" of a modern pencil is not made of lead at all. It is actually a mixture of graphite (a form of carbon) and clay. The more clay the lead contains, the harder it is.

Building With Soil

Soil has always been used to make building materials. At first, people used earth or mud for building. Then they made mud bricks. They learned how to make clay bricks as hard as stone by firing (heating) them at a high temperature. Today, we still use raw materials from the ground to make bricks, concrete, and glass. As usual, nature got there first. Some creatures make homes by tunneling into soil. Others stick soil or mud together to build nests. Without soil to provide these materials, we would have to build with stones, and a lot of creatures would be homeless!

HOUSES IN ANCIENT EGYPT were made from mud bricks. The mud was collected from the Nile River. Chopped straw was often mixed with it to strengthen it. The mud was molded into brick shapes using a wooden frame. They were then dried in the Sun.

Only another 2,000 bricks to go!

14

Wattle and daub is a clever building material. Wattle on its own is bendy and drafty. Daub is weak and cracks easily. But together, they strengthen each other and make a tough, weather-proof material.

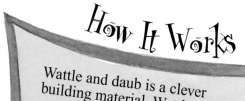

ONE WAY to build a wall is to slap mud on a screen of woven twigs. It's called wattle and daub. Wattle is the wooden screen and daub is the mud. Straw and animal dung may also be mixed with the mud.

THE GLASS that covers modern skyscrapers is made from sand. Without sand or glass, what would skyscrapers look like? What would we make windows from?

INSECTS such as ants and termites use soil to make their homes. Some termites stick soil together to build giant homes like insect skyscrapers.

SOME BIRDS, such as swallows and martins, build their nests from mud. They scoop up the mud in their beaks, mix it with spit, and then mold it into a nest shape.

Covering Up

Soil is useful for burying things that need to be hidden. All sorts of pipes and cables are kept out of sight by being put underground. Without soil, they would all be on the surface. A lot of people choose to be buried when they die. If there were no soil, we wouldn't be able to bury bodies. The remains of many ancient civilizations have become buried, allowing later civilizations to discover them. We also find coins and valuables buried by people long ago. Without soil, none of these things would survive for us to discover.

WEALTHY PEOPLE in the ancient world had no banks or safes to keep their money and valuables in. They hid important things by burying them in the ground, often in clay pots. If they weren't dug up again, archaeologists sometimes found them hundreds or thousands of years later. These buried valuables are called hoards.

WE THROW AWAY an enormous amount of trash every year. Most of it is buried in the ground and covered with a deep layer of topsoil. If there were no soil to cover the trash, our towns and cities would be surrounded by ugly mountains of smelly, rotting waste.

WE KNOW A LOT about people who lived long ago, because we have dug up lots of things they left behind, including their skeletons! Soil keeps bones and belongings safely together until archaeologists find them.

A NETWORK of pipes and cables connects our homes to essential power, gas, water, telephone, and waste services. All of these pipes and cables are usually kept out of sight, underground. Imagine if there were no soil to cover them!

WATERLOGGED SOIL preserves anything buried in it, including human bodies. Tollund Man, a body found in a bog in Denmark, looks as if he is sleeping and might wake up at any moment. In fact, he died 2,300 years ago.

Growing Plants

In almost every place on Earth where there is soil, there are plants, too. Without soil, there would be no grass, or bushes, or flowers, or trees, because they all need soil. Plants send roots down into the soil to take up water and the nutrients dissolved in it. The roots also anchor the plants in the ground, enabling them to stand up. When crops are grown in the same ground year after year, they quickly use up all the nutrients in the soil. Over time, the organic matter in the soil breaks down, too. Farmers are able to keep growing crops on the same fields because they replace the nutrients and organic matter in the soil. One common farm fertilizer that has lots of organic matter in it is animal waste, but spreading it over the fields can be very smelly!

TREE ROOTS fan out at least as far underground as the branches spread above ground. Roots are usually close to the surface, but in dry parts of the world some roots travel 200 feet (60 meters) underground to find water.

TALL TREES and other plants can stand up only because of their network of roots below the soil. The roots reach down into the ground and grip it like hundreds of long fingers. You can see some of them when a tree is blown over in a storm.

Fill two pots with sand. Plant apple seeds in each pot. Add water to one pot only. Water the other pot with cold tea. The plants feeding on the tea should grow better, as tea leaves contain nutrients that act as a natural fertilizer.

That stinks!

LUSH GREEN rain forests look as if they must be growing on rich, fertile soil. Surprisingly, rain forest soil is very poor. When plants die and decay, living plants take up their nutrients so quickly that they don't build up in the soil.

SOIL IS VITAL for the world's food supply. The crops that feed 7 billion people on Earth are grown on about one tenth of all the land. Without soil, there would be no crops or grass to feed the animals we eat.

19

Fuel From Soil

The way we live today is possible because of soil that formed long before the first humans walked on Earth. Millions of years ago, during the era of the dinosaurs and even before that, plants were sometimes buried under mud in swampy areas. Buried plants didn't rot in the open air and weren't eaten by animals. Over time, more and more soil built up on top of the dead plants. The weight of all the soil squashed the plants and pushed them deeper and deeper underground. The soil itself gradually changed into rock. Heat and pressure changed the thick layers of dead plants underneath into coal. Without that ancient soil, we wouldn't have coal today or any of the electricity that is made by burning coal.

ANOTHER FUEL that comes from soil is peat. Peat contains so much organic matter that it can be dried and burned like coal. Blocks of peat are cut from bogs in places like Ireland and Finland. They are then piled up in heaps and left to dry in the sunshine.

COAL HAS BEEN collected and burned to provide heat for thousands of years. At first, people collected coal washed up from the seabed onto beaches, especially after a storm. Sea coal is still collected today in some places.

Why does buried vegetation turn into coal instead of rotting? Many organisms that rot vegetation need oxygen from the air or water. Burying the vegetation keeps air out, so it doesn't rot. Over time, heat and pressure change it into coal.

COAL STORES energy from the Sun taken in by plants that lived millions of years ago. The lump of coal you burn today may have started its life in a flooded forest growing when dinosaurs still roamed Earth.

COAL CAN still be found on some beaches. Waves pound the coal and break it down into gritty little pieces. The coal forms a black layer on top of the sand.

COAL FORMS thick layers called seams. Some coal seams lie near the surface, but many are deep underground. Miners dig shafts and tunnels to reach these deep seams and cut the coal out. The first miners used hand tools. Giant cutting machines are used today.

Look Out!

Soil is usually steady and stable, but sometimes it moves, with disastrous results. Soil can be moved by earthquakes, floods, waves, droughts, and even the weight of buildings standing on top of it. An earthquake can shake soil free from a slope and cause a landslide. Water and waves can cause landslides, too. Floods can wash soil away. The soil underneath a building can settle (sink), pressed down by the building's weight. Modern buildings have deep foundations to try to prevent some of these problems from occurring.

THE LEANING Tower of Pisa in Italy leans because the ground underneath it settled more on one side than on the other side.

I think I need glasses – that tower looks a bit crooked to me!

WATER is often to blame for landslides. Underground springs or heavy rain can fill all the spaces inside soil with water. This can make the layers of soil so slippery that one layer eventually breaks free and slides down the hill.

LANDSLIDES are common along coastal cliffs. Waves pound the base of a cliff and wash earth away. Eventually, there is nothing holding up the cliff edge and it collapses into the sea.

Top Tip

Never walk near the edge of a clifftop—the ground could suddenly give way and collapse. Stay away from the bottom of cliffs for the same reason.

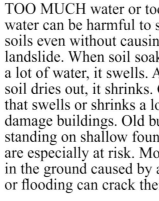

WHEN AN EARTHQUAKE shakes wet ground, the soil loses its strength and behaves like quicksand. It can't support the weight of buildings, which sink into the ground, often leaning over at crazy angles. This strange effect is called liquefaction.

TOO MUCH water or too little water can be harmful to some soils even without causing a landslide. When soil soaks up a lot of water, it swells. As the soil dries out, it shrinks. Ground that swells or shrinks a lot can damage buildings. Old buildings standing on shallow foundations are especially at risk. Movements in the ground caused by a drought or flooding can crack their walls.

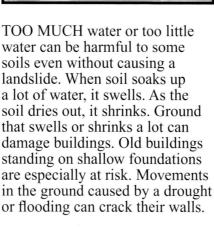

Losing Soil

Soil is a limited resource and it is in danger. Soil is being lost from the land all the time. In some places, the sea is washing it away. This is called coastal erosion. Heavy rain and floods wash it away into rivers, too.

When a long drought dries out the land, the dusty topsoil can be picked up by the wind and blown away. This is called wind erosion. As the population of the world continues to grow, more and more soil is disappearing under new buildings and roads. Soil can also be lost due to poor farming methods that remove valuable nutrients and organic matter.

THE LONG DROUGHT in the United States in the 1930s was called the Dust Bowl. It made the ground so dry that millions of tons of precious farm soil turned to dust and blew away. So much soil was stripped off the land that the sky was often blackened by vast dust storms that turned day into night.

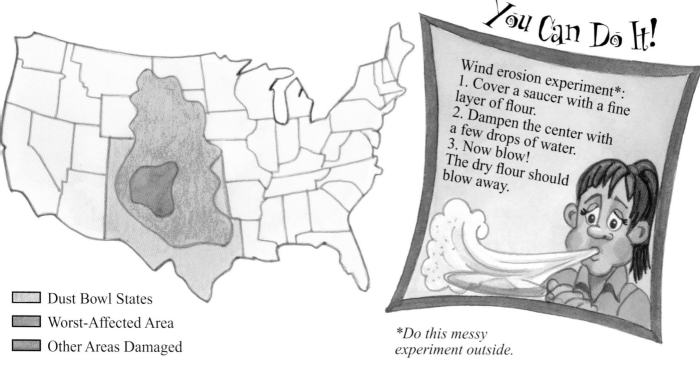

Dust Bowl States

Worst-Affected Area

Other Areas Damaged

Wind erosion experiment*:
1. Cover a saucer with a fine layer of flour.
2. Dampen the center with a few drops of water.
3. Now blow! The dry flour should blow away.

*Do this messy experiment outside.

THE DUST BOWL put thousands of farms and ranches out of business across America's Great Plains. About three million people moved out of the affected states to search for work elsewhere. They were known as "Okies" because many of them came from Oklahoma. The drought came to an end when regular rainfall finally returned after 1940.

LAND IS FALLING into the sea in some places, such as the coast of California and the east coast of England. Sometimes, so much land is lost that people's homes teeter on the edge, before one more storm sends them falling into the sea. Some important buildings have been rescued from disaster by being picked up and moved back from the edge.

Health and Beauty

Did you know that some products you use every day contain substances from soil that help to keep you healthy? Some widely used antibiotics (bacteria-killing medicines) were discovered by people studying soil and are used to treat infections. Clay is used in some medicines, too. Animals discovered the health effects of soil long ago. Some creatures eat clay to help their digestion. Clay is also used to make some beauty products, such as face masks. Without soil, there would be a lot more stomachaches and we'd have to find another way to make many of the health and beauty products that we use today.

MUD MASKS can be used to cleanse the skin. They remove oil and add moisture. The smooth, fine-grained clay is spread on the face and left to dry. It can look a bit strange!

Is it working?

BACTERIA IN SOIL are very good at fighting one another, so soil is a good place for scientists to look for new antibiotics. In 2015, a new antibiotic called teixobactin was discovered. Lots of bacteria in soil still need to be studied, so there might be more medicines made from soil in the future.

How It Works

Clay is very good at mopping up liquid because its particles are very small and there are lots of tiny spaces called pores between them. Liquid soaks into the particles and fills up the pores.

SOME PARROTS in South America eat clay. This enables them to eat poisonous seeds, because the clay soaks up the poison and stops it from harming the parrots.

SOME TOOTHPASTES contain a fine, white powdered clay called china clay. It's the same clay that is used to make china dishware. The clay helps to scrub teeth clean and remove stains. It also helps to make some toothpastes creamy.

CLAY is often used in medicines you might take for an upset stomach. It helps to soothe the stomach because just like the clay eaten by the parrots, it absorbs (soaks up) harmful substances.

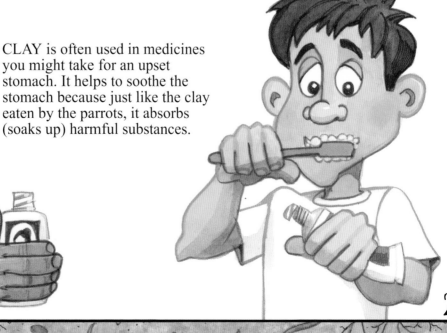

27

Looking to the Future

Soil was often not valued enough in the past. It seemed like an endless supply of dirt. Now we know that it's actually a valuable resource that we must protect. In the future, we will have to use soil more efficiently to produce enough food for the growing population. We will also need to protect soil from pollution. Most scientists believe that our climate is changing because the world is warming. They predict that this will change our weather on a global scale, especially rainfall and temperature. In the future, farmers may have to adapt to these changes by altering their farming methods.

FOR THOUSANDS of years farmers have plowed their soil to make it ready for new crops. However, the familiar sight of plowed fields may disappear from future farms. Plowing dries soil, destroys worm tunnels, and kills some of the organisms that live in soil. A different method called no-till farming avoids plowing altogether.

NATURE takes a long time to make soil. Instead of waiting hundreds of years for nature to do the job, scientists are looking for ways to make artificial soil. Then they could make as much as they need when they need it. One of these artificial soils is made from the coal ash from power stations mixed with sewage sludge, the thick mud produced when wastewater is treated (cleaned).

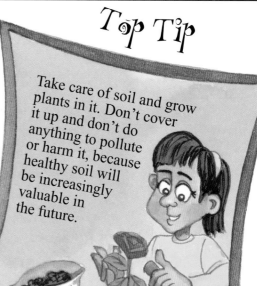

Top Tip

Take care of soil and grow plants in it. Don't cover it up and don't do anything to pollute or harm it, because healthy soil will be increasingly valuable in the future.

OUR CHANGING CLIMATE may alter the nutrients, organic matter, or living organisms in soil. Climate change could produce excess rainfall and floods in some places and long droughts in other places. Farmers may have to grow different crops in the future to suit the changing climate.

FUTURE SPACE TRAVELERS who land on other planets, such as Mars, will not be able take enough food with them for their long journey. Food is simply too heavy. The astronauts will have to produce their own food by growing plants. Soil is too heavy to take with them, so they may have to make their own soil from the planet's dry, dusty surface, called regolith. Perhaps they could take dried sewage sludge with them and mix it with the regolith and water.

Glossary

Antibiotics Substances that kill bacteria.

Artificial Made by people, not occurring in nature.

Bacteria Microscopic organisms, each made of only one living cell.

Bedrock Solid rock that forms the earth's surface.

Bog Waterlogged ground containing a lot of plant material, especially moss.

Clay Fine-grained sticky earth that can be molded when wet.

Climate Weather conditions over a long period of time—decades or centuries.

Earth Another word for soil; also the name of the planet we live on.

Fertilizer A substance containing nutrients or organic matter that is mixed with soil to make it more fertile (able to grow more plants).

Firing Baking clay at a very high temperature to harden it.

Foundations The lowest part of a building, usually underground.

Fungi Organisms such as mushrooms, toadstools, and molds that have no roots or leaves and grow from spores.

Geologist A scientist who studies the history of Earth, how it formed, and what it is made of.

Glacier A river of ice slowly sliding downhill.

Grit Small particles of sand or rock.

Humus Organic matter in soil, containing the remains of dead plants.

Minerals The many substances that rock is made of.

Nematode One of the many tiny worms that live in soil. They range in size from a period on this page to about 0.09 of an inch (2.5 millimeters).

Nutrients Minerals dissolved in soil water that are taken up by the roots of a plant and used as food.

Organic A description of living matter or matter that was once alive.

Organism A living plant or animal.

Pigment A substance that gives paint, ink, or another material its color. Some natural pigments are made by grinding up earth or rock to make a fine powder. Others are made from plants or insects.

Pollution Unwanted, harmful substances in the environment.

Population The number of plants or animals living in a place or region.

Pore A tiny opening that gas or liquid can pass through.

Protozoa Microscopic single-celled animals.

Raw materials Basic substances that products are made from.

Resource A supply of materials. Soil is a natural resource.

Sand Loose grains of rock bigger than those of silt or clay.

Silt Fine grains of rock bigger than those of clay and smaller than sand.

States of matter Different types of matter. The three that we find most often in everyday life are solid, liquid, and gas. Another, called plasma, is found in stars.

Stone Age The period of history from more than three million years ago to about 8,000 years ago.

Termites Ant-like insects. Some termites build giant nests from soil.

Toxic Poisonous.

Virus A tiny particle of genetic material that can invade living cells and use them to make many more copies of itself.

Index

Top Soil Scientists

Charles Darwin (1809–1882)
Darwin is famous for his theory of evolution, but he also spent 40 years studying earthworms. He found that they help to break down organic matter in soil by passing it through the body and digesting it. He also found that their tunnels aerate (let air in) the soil. He observed worms pulling leaves down into their tunnels. He wrote a book about it, called *The Formation of Vegetable Mould Through the Action of Worms, With Observations of Their Habits*. It was a best seller!

Vasily Dokuchaev (1846–1903)
Dokuchaev is the Russian scientist known as the father of soil science. He set up the first department of soil science in Russia and led expeditions to study soil in different parts of Russia. He was the first person to say that soil was formed not only by the rock beneath it, but also by the action of climate, vegetation, place, and time. A crater on Mars is named after him.

Curtis F. Marbut (1863–1935)
After earning degrees from the University of Missouri and Harvard University, Marbut taught geology at the University of Missouri until 1910. Then he went to work as a soil scientist for the U.S. Bureau of Soils. While he was there, he developed the first system for dividing U.S. soils into different types.

Plants Without Soil

Did you know that it's possible to grow plants without soil? Plants can be grown in gravel or a similar substance called growing medium. Water, with plant food dissolved in it, is pumped through the growing medium. The roots of the plants spread through the growing medium and take up the nutrient-rich water. This way of growing plants is called hydroponics. Hydroponics is more costly than growing plants in soil, but it could be used more in the future if there is not enough good soil for growing crops.

Making Fossils

Without soil, we would know very little about dinosaurs and other animals that lived millions of years ago. Fossils are the remains of these ancient creatures. Most of the creatures that died millions of years ago were eaten or simply decayed and disappeared, but some were buried quickly by landslides, or by ash from erupting volcanoes. Bacteria broke down the soft parts of the creatures, leaving the bones behind. The bones soaked up water in the ground. Minerals in the water slowly replaced the bones, changing them into fossils. Over time, more and more soil, mud, or ash buried the fossils deeper. The huge weight of the ground pressing down eventually changed the earth around the fossils to rock. If weather slowly wears away the rock, then millions of years later a sharp-eyed fossil hunter might spot the fossils emerging.